LORDE

Heidi
Krumenauer

PURPLE TOAD
PUBLISHING

Printing   1   2   3   4   5   6   7   8   9

A Beacon Biography

Big Time Rush
Carly Rae Jepsen
Drake
Harry Styles of One Direction
Jennifer Lawrence
Kevin Durant
Lorde
Markus "Notch" Persson, Creator of *Minecraft*
Neil deGrasse Tyson
Peyton Manning
Robert Griffin III (RG3)

Publisher's Cataloging-in-Publication Data
Krumenauer, Heidi
    Lorde / written by Heidi Krumenauer.
        p. cm.
            Includes bibliographic references.
            ISBN 9781624691225
1. Lorde, 1996–Juvenile literature. 2. Singers — New Zealand — Biography — Juvenile literature. I. Series: Beacon Biographies Collection Two.
  ML3930 2015
  782.0092
                                                            Library of Congress Control Number: 2014945170

eBook ISBN: 9781624691232

ABOUT THE AUTHOR: Heidi Krumenauer has written more than 1,200 newspaper and magazine articles. Her first book, *Why Does Grandma Have a Wibble?*, was published in 2007. She is also the author of several celebrity biographies, including *Lady Gaga* and *Harry Styles of One Direction*. Krumenauer graduated from the University of Wisconsin-Platteville in 1991 with a degree in Technical Communications Management. She holds a position in upper management with a Fortune 400 insurance company. She and her husband, Jeff, raise their two sons, Noah and Payton, in Southern Wisconsin.

PUBLISHER'S NOTE: The data in this book has been researched in depth, and to the best of our knowledge is factual. Although every measure is taken to give an accurate account, Purple Toad Publishing makes no warranty of the accuracy of the information and is not liable for damages caused by inaccuracies. This story has not been authorized or endorsed by Lorde.

CONTENTS

Lorde became the first New Zealand solo artist ever to top the U.S. singles chart when "Royals" hit No. 1 on Billboard's Hot 100.

Who Are You Calling Racist?

In the vast world of music there are highs and lows, and sometimes they happen all at once. Shortly after Lorde burst onto the music scene in the summer of 2013 with her mega hit, "Royals," Veronica Bayette Flores called Lorde's lyrics "deeply racist" in her October 2013 blog titled *Feministing.* She felt that Lorde was putting down black people and rappers.

The offending lyrics, according to Flores, are:

My friends and I—we've cracked the code,
We count our dollars on the train to the party.
And everyone who knows us knows that we're fine with this,
We didn't come from money.

But every song's like gold teeth, grey goose, trippin' in the bathroom,
Blood stains, ball gowns, trashin' the hotel room,
We don't care, we're driving Cadillacs in our dreams.
But everybody's like Cristal, Maybach, diamonds on your time piece.

Jet planes, islands, tigers on a gold leash,
We don't care, we aren't caught up in your love affair.

By 2014, Lorde triumphed over critics of her song "Royals" as the music industry awarded her with the Song of the Year award as well as the Best Female Pop Vocal award.

"While I love a good critique of wealth accumulation and inequity, this song is not one; in fact, it is deeply racist," Flores says in her blog. "Because we all know who she's [Lorde's] thinking when we're talking gold teeth, Cristal, and Maybachs. Why aren't we critiquing wealth by taking hits at golf or polo or Central Park East?"

Flores' strong opinion prompted other large media outlets to start asking the same questions about potential racism in the song's lyrics.

Lorde's fans were not happy with Flores' accusations and neither were some outspoken media voices. New Zealand journalist Lynda Brendish said, "I realize not everything in this world is an instrument of oppression. And not everything in this world should be viewed through the lens of Americans, particularly when it comes to race and cultures of other countries. To insist otherwise is ignorant at best and imperialistic at worst."

Lynda Brendish

While countries across the world were engaged in a deep racism debate, what was Lorde thinking? "I was just sort of reeling off some of the things which are commonly mentioned in hip-hop and the Top 40. I did get a little ridiculous on it, but the sentiment's there," she said in an interview with National Public Radio. "I've always loved hip-hop, but as a fan of hip-hop, I've always had to kind of suspend disbelief because, obviously, I don't have a Bentley. There's a distance between that and the life I have with my friends going to parties and getting public transport and doing the things that every other teenager does."

Bloggers and journalists can interpret the song's meaning any way they choose, but Lorde stated in a May 2013 interview with *The Cut,* "I've always listened to a lot of rap. It's all, look at this car that cost me so much money, look at this Champagne. When I was going out with my friends, we would raid someone's freezer at [her] parents' house because we didn't have enough money to get dinner. I experienced this disconnect. Everyone knows it's B.S., but someone has to write about it."

More than 1.3 million people call the big city of Auckland, New Zealand, home. Lorde grew up in the much smaller suburb of Auckland called Devonport, which along with its neighboring town, have a combined population of roughly 5,500 residents.

Chapter 2

Becoming Lorde

Ella Yelich-O'Connor was born in Auckland, New Zealand, on November 7, 1996, to parents, Vic O'Connor and Sonja Yelich. Ella's father is a civil engineer and her mother is a prize-winning New Zealand poet. Ella has three siblings; an older sister, a younger sister, and a younger brother.

Ella was raised in Devonport, a seaside suburb of Auckland, New Zealand's most populous city. Devonport is known to the locals as "the Bubble" because it is so closed off from everything around it. Ella describes her hometown as "the kind of suburb that people make movies about."

Early on, Ella was influenced by the music of Neil Young, Fleetwood Mac, and Etta James. With her mother's love of writing, Ella was never far from books. Her mother brought her books to read, and that is how she became a fan of the short fiction works of Raymond Carver. "Mum always made sure there were lots of books around. For a long time we had a TV but no DVD player. Then Mum got one but she only allowed us to watch old stuff like *Wonder Woman*, *The Partridge Family* and *Little House on the Prairie*," she said.

Ella began performing musical theater when she was five years old. Being used to crowds, Ella wasn't shy about competing in her school's speech competitions. In 2007, she won the North Shore Primary Schools' Speech competition, representing Vauxhall School.

In 2008, she and her classmates at Belmont Intermediate competed in the Kids' Lit Quiz, but they didn't win. Because of that, they missed out on a trip to Oxford, England, to compete on an international level. Ella told the local newspaper, "We're really glad but we're really annoyed we couldn't go to Oxford. We'll be back next year." She was right. The next year her team competed and placed second in the world final held in South Africa.

In the same year, 12-year-old Ella's life changed forever. A&R talent executive, Scott Maclachlan, saw a video of her performing Duffy's "Warwick Avenue" in a school concert at Belmont and contacted her.

Scott was impressed and quickly signed Ella to the Universal record label. When Universal suggested that she make an album of soul remakes, she refused. Ella wanted to write her own music, although she had never done that before. Her only experience in writing came in the form of short stories. Interestingly, Universal listened to young Ella's demands. "They were pretty open-minded about it. They got straight away that I was a bit weird, that I would not be doing anything I didn't want to do, and they completely went

with that," she told Alexis Petridis of *The Guardian*. "Maybe it was because the record company was in New Zealand. It's cool that they were cool with that, because if they hadn't been, it wouldn't have been a very good outcome."

Ella's manager, Scott Maclachlan, travels all over the world with her, handling her busy schedule.

Ella and Louis McDonald performed acoustic musical arrangements at The Vic Unplugged in 2010 as part of a week-long celebration to mark the opening of the refurbished Victoria Theatre in Devonport (now renamed as the Victoria Picture Palace and Theatre).

Ella started writing songs on her guitar at the age of 12 or 13—she doesn't remember exactly when it started. She does remember that the more she wrote, the better she became. "The music-making process was very, very casual in the beginning because I was only 12 and didn't know what I wanted to do," she told *The Daily Beast.* "I took singing lessons and started working with songwriters in a very casual setting—trying to find someone and a sound I could click with."

Universal teamed Ella up with several song writers over the course of two years, hoping to find a style that would work, but something was always missing. Two years of trying to get it right turned into success when producer Joel Little showed up to work with Ella. Together they wrote 10 songs for her debut EP (Extended Play) "The Love Club," which released on March 8, 2013. That EP also launched the song "Royals" that would quickly make her name a household word. But she wouldn't do it with the name Ella Yelich-O'Connor. To the world, she would now be known as Lorde.

Lorde has been an avid reader since childhood. At age 14, she helped proofread her mother Sonja's master's thesis.

The Rise of "Royals"

Lorde wrote the song "Royals" in July 2012 during her school's summer break. It was partly inspired by the album *Watch the Throne* by Jay-Z and Kanye West. "I really enjoyed it," she said. "I can get absorbed in Kanye's world...all the crazy extravagances he's talking about. And I started listening to a lot more top-40 music, and realized a lot of the stuff isn't very relatable to anyone's lives."

Lorde took her lyrics to her co-writer and producer Joel Little. "We spent a couple days doing the music and recording the demo, which is super-similar to the version we ended up putting out. We worked on a bunch of stuff that week and 'Royals' felt cool, but it didn't feel like a smash or anything like that."

She was wrong. It was a smash! When "Royals" released in March 2013, it debuted at number one on the New Zealand charts, where it remained for three weeks. Even with the success in New Zealand, Lorde wasn't confident that it would be received with the same love in the United States. During one week in October 2013, "Royals" was played 835,000 times on SoundCloud, an online platform that allows users to upload, record, and promote their originally-created music. During that same week, Lorde's official "Royals" video received almost 2 million views on YouTube.

It was plain to see that the world was catching "'Royals" fever. It was used as the soundtrack for the 2013 Wimbledon Championships and was covered by contestants on the X-Factor reality television competition. During the summer of 2013, Lorde gained the attention of mega pop star, Katy Perry, who invited Lorde to join her world tour as an opening act. Lorde told Samantha Hayes of *3rd Degree* that she turned down Perry's offer. "I have a pretty good gut instinct for stuff and if it feels right I'll do it," she said.

Perry had no hard feelings. She told TVNZ that she's always on the lookout for new artists. "I love Lorde. I love her sensibility. I love her lyrics; I think they're really important for this time right now in pop culture because she brings some real substance and is thought-provoking. She shakes things up a little bit, and we need that. I love a 16-year-old girl with a mind."

With a mega recording like "Royals," it would be easy to assume that the name 'Lorde' comes from a long line of aristocrats, but that's not the case. Lorde told *The Huffington Post,* "When I was trying to come up with a stage name, I thought 'Lord' was super rad, but really masculine. Ever since I was a little kid, I have been really into royals and aristocracy. So to make Lord more feminine, I just put an 'e' on the end! Some people think it's religious, but it's not."

At home or at school, Lorde still answers to 'Ella'. "My name is Ella. That's who I am at school, hanging out with friends, while I'm doing homework," she told *Interview magazine.* "But when I'm up on stage, Lorde is a character. My friends actually find that really difficult to digest, separating me from the theatrical character they see on stage; but they're getting used to it. People that were close to me before the music came out are still close to me."

Some of those friends, no doubt, have spent time shopping with Lorde in New Zealand. "I've always loved clothes," she told *Teen Vogue.* "I'm not super clued up on brands, because it's expensive! But I love clothes...and I'm always looking at stuff I want to get or want to try to make." Growing up, Lorde didn't have much money to spend on nice clothes. Instead, she and her friends went "opp shopping"—short for "opportunity shopping"—as she calls it. "It's like thrift stores. It's called that because the stores are run by churches. So we get lots of vintage clothes. It's cool."

Lorde loves to dress up like a lady in long, classic gowns, but lately she's become fond of wearing pants. "I've never really worn pants before, but now I just want to wear pants all the time!" On stage, Lorde loves to flaunt a long dress, but loves chunky sneakers, too. "That's what stage wear is about for me—I've got to feel strong and feel like I can command attention."

Vanity Fair *magazine called Lorde the "Queen of Darkness" in January 2014, because of her dark hair, dark clothes, and dark vibe. "I like simple clothes," Lorde said. "But sometimes I'll go for a goth-witch vibe."*

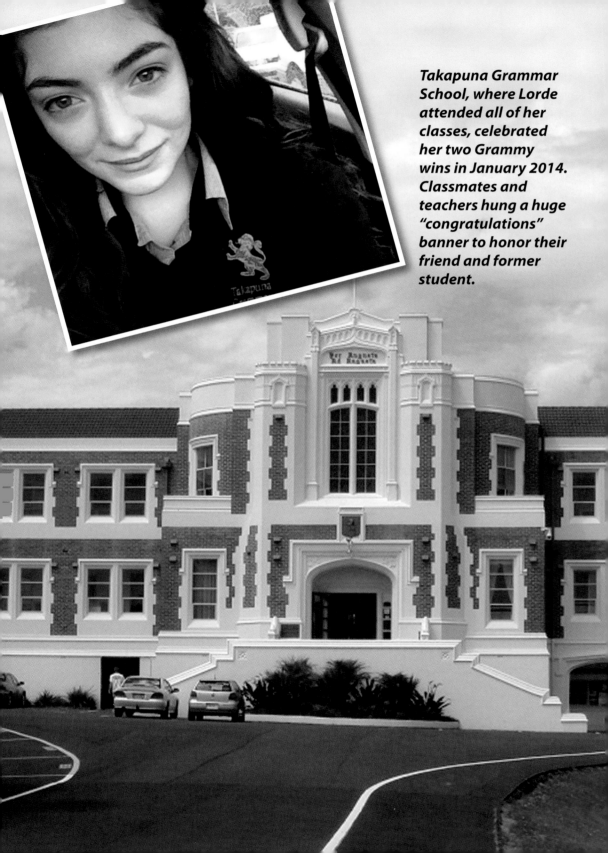

Takapuna Grammar School, where Lorde attended all of her classes, celebrated her two Grammy wins in January 2014. Classmates and teachers hung a huge "congratulations" banner to honor their friend and former student.

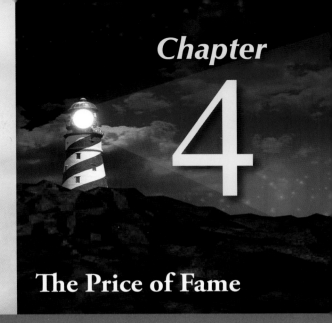

Early in her music career, Lorde remained a student at Takapuna Grammar School in Belmont, Auckland. No different than other teenagers, she liked to socialize with her friends, which distracted her from her studies. "My mum takes my iPhone off me at night because I need to do homework and sleep, otherwise I'd spend all night on Facebook and Instagram."

At the age of 16, in her second-to-last year of school, Ella considered her future in music and pursuing a higher degree in academics. "I love learning, but at the same time I love being in the studio and learning new things there. If I do decide to leave school at the end of this year, that's a bridge we'll cross. But I do, one day, still really want to go to University to study media and film probably."

As publicity demands, performances and writing music continue to consume Lorde's time, she may need to reconsider her academic goals. With more than a year of high school remaining, Lorde admitted to Rolling Stone that she hadn't been to class in a while. "I don't know how school's going to go," she said. She's not sure when, or if, she'll graduate, and has no specific college plans. "I read and write so much anyway, I don't feel I'm particularly missing out."

On June 16, 2014, Lorde tweeted, "BEST DAY". Went to Niagara Falls - my dad proposed to my mum after almost 30 years together." Lorde's father, Vic, proposed to her mother, Sonja, at Niagra Falls.

She told *3rd Degree* that she was getting used to the life of a pop star, and was starting to enjoy it, and even admitted that performing was far better than attending school. "This feels like normality. I love it. I get to do these crazy things a lot of people wouldn't normally get to do."

In the beginning of her career, Lorde took great steps to maintain some anonymity. She liked her privacy, but the public wanted to know what she was doing. Even more than that, they wanted to know what she looked like. "I could feel people getting aggressive, like, show yourself already," she told *The Cut*. "I mean, I understand. I write pop music. People aren't used to not being able to put a face or a body to it. So I was like, all right."

It didn't take long for Lorde to recognize that her new life of fame isn't perfect all the time. "Sometimes I feel so lonely I don't want to do it anymore. But truth is, I love what I do so much. I've never been so happy, or worked so hard." Still, her appearances have gotten in the way of birthday parties and hanging out with friends. Her alarm clock buzzes at 4 a.m. so she can start working. She can't walk down the street without people wanting to take pictures of her having private

Lorde accomplished what many have not—she graced the cover of Rolling Stone magazine at the age of 17! To make sure she looked her best, Lorde worked with celebrity hairstylist Jen Atkin and makeup artist Robin Black.

When Lorde is on stage, her signature dark makeup looks flawless, but in February 2014, she showed her fans that she's just a normal teenager. She posted a selfie to Instagram showing her true, unedited acne-fighting skin and messy hair in a bun. She wrote, "In bed in Paris with my acne cream on."

Two photos from the same concert show how the magic of Photoshop can remove Lorde's blemishes. The photo on the bottom is untouched. Lorde tweeted about the photos, "i find this curious - two photos from today, one edited so my skin is perfect and one real. remember flaws are ok :-) ."

time with her boyfriend. "I get recognized, which is weird, when I'm at a restaurant and I've got my mouth full of food. But for the most part, people are really kind. My friends don't treat me any differently."

It's not just her fans who have been taking an interest in her. Celebrities have shown their support on Twitter. Referring to her new star status, Lorde told *Women's Wear Daily* in August 2013, "All these people tweeting about me is probably the biggest indicator." Included in that long list are Selena Gomez and Jamie Lynn Spears, but Lorde is most amused with Backstreet Boys. "I was having a conversation with a bunch of friends and just said [on Twitter], 'I want to write a boy band hit.' And [the Backstreet Boys] were like, 'You should. We would sing it!'"

In all seriousness, Lorde thinks about the musicians she'd like to sing with in the future. In a Q&A session with *The New York Times*, Lorde said, "There are obviously all sorts of people I think are super-talented, but I kind of want to work with Pharrell. I think it would be fun."

Working with others is part of the business for Lorde, and it's also a piece that she finds most challenging. "Sometimes it can be hard not to let record company dudes turn things to crap. Or bad stylists, or music video directors who don't get it," Lorde said in her blog. "Everyday I turn down countless requests from TV shows and brands and films that want to use my music to sell their product, because I don't feel that they're right. If I'd granted every sandwich chain and skincare brand and coming-of-age blockbuster use of my songs, I'd probably be a millionaire, but I'm extremely fussy."

"Every situation I'm in, I'm thinking about lyrics," says Lorde. "I'll be at a party and enjoying it, but at the same time looking around and thinking about the translation, and how I'll write about it. You can never shut that off as a writer."

Chapter

5

Staying Grounded

Lorde keeps a quote from author William S. Burroughs close to her as she makes decisions that affect the future of her music: "Build a good name for yourself, because eventually that will become your currency."

"That has always stuck with me, and every step that I've taken since I signed my development deal has been to ensure I am exactly who I want to be, and perceived how I'd like to be perceived," she said. Lorde admits that being a teenage girl is difficult in the music business because people would rather talk to her manager than her. "This usually lasts all of 10 minutes, until I insert the kind of dry sentence that makes most adults splutter and blush and reach for their water, and after this they start taking me seriously."

While she needs to be a bit tough in the industry to make sure that her voice is heard, Lorde still remembers her place at home. When she returned from the New Zealand Music Awards, her mother said, "Remember your place at the table." Lorde told Hermione Hoby of *The Observer*, "I come from a large family and often there'll be eight or 10 of us eating. So it's a thing at our house to have the adults sitting at one end of the table and, the younger you

Lorde loves her fans, but she is very firm on a decision to never give them a cheesy nickname. "I find it grating to lump everyone into a really awkward, pun-centric name. People joke about it on Twitter, 'You should call us The Disciples.' Never! I have discouraged it. I've tweeted multiple times, 'No fan name, I do not condone this.'"

are, the farther down the table you sit. So she was saying, you might be kind of a big shot out there, but here you still have to sit down at that end. Which is, I think, a nice way of keeping grounded."

Being grounded also means that Lorde has taken an interest in others' tragedies and has found a way to help. She joined other big name music artists like One Direction, Beyoncé, Justin Bieber, and Justin Timberlake on a special compilation released in November 2013. Money raised from Songs for the Philippines, available on iTunes, will benefit people affected by Typhoon Haiyan. Lorde's song "The Love Club," is featured on the compilation. It came on the heals of the release of Lorde's debut album, *Pure Heroine,* on September 27, 2013. Several of the album's songs were originally released on *The Love Club* EP (Extended Play) early in 2013. To no one's surprise, *Pure Heroine* received positive reviews from the music critics and Lorde fans.

So, what does it feel like to be a big shot in the music industry? "I'm not gonna lie, it's pretty cool," Lorde says. "I'm pretty stoked. My opinion on what is normal changes all the time. But yes, it feels really good." And it should feel good! According to Billboard.com, on her 17th birthday, Lorde signed a deal with Songs Music Publishing, Inc., that was reportedly worth $2.5 million.

Lorde's boyfriend, James Lowe, is a successful photographer. He often takes photos of his girlfriend and posts them to Instagram. One caption he wrote of Lorde said, "Still no words . . . so proud."

Lorde performed on Day 1 of the three-day Lollapalooza event at Grant Park on August 1, 2014, in Chicago.

Can you top that? Maybe. Just a week later, Lorde was named one of *Time* magazine's Top 16 Most Influential Teenagers. And there's more! Earlier in August, Lorde became the youngest woman in 17 years to top Billboard's Top Alternative songs chart. In October, Lorde jointly won the 2013 Silver Scroll Award for "Royals," which is an achievement in original New Zealand pop songwriting. She was also nominated for four Grammys for the 56th Annual Grammy Awards for Record of the Year and Song of the Year for "Royals" and Best Pop Vocal Album for *Pure Heroine.*

While most teenagers are studying for exams and preparing for life after high school, this New Zealand teen has just tapped into what appears to be a long musical career!

" 'Build a good name for yourself, because eventually that will become your currency.'

That has always stuck with me, and every step that I've taken since I signed my development deal has been to ensure I am exactly who I want to be, and perceived how I'd like to be perceived."

—Lorde

Fans sat outside the gates for several hours before Lorde was due to perform on the stage of the ACL Music Festival in Austin, Texas, in October 2014.

1996	Ella Yelich-O'Connor is born to Vic O'Connor and Sonja Yelich on November 7.
2007	Ella wins the North Shore Primary Schools' Speech competition.
2008	Ella is discovered by A&R talent executive, Scott Maclachlan of Universal Music. She signs with Universal.
2009	Ella and her classmates place second in the Kids' Lit Quiz world final held in South Africa.
2013	Lorde signs a $2.5 million record deal with Songs Music Publishing, Inc. Lorde's first major release, *The Love Club* EP, was released in March. Lorde releases her debut single "Royals" in June. It peaks at number one on the US Billboard Hot 100. She is named among *Time* magazine's most influential teenagers in the world. Lorde starts dating photographer, James Lowe.
2014	Lorde announces her North American tour. Lorde ranks in the *Forbes* "30 Under 30" list. Lorde embarks on a tour that covers North America. She also performs around the world, in countries including Australia, Chile, Argentina, and Brazil. In June, she releases a two-piece make-up limited edition collection with MAC Cosmetics, consisting of a lipstick and eyeliner. In September, Lorde releases "Yellow Flicker Beat" as the first single from the soundtrack album for the film *The Hunger Games: Mockingjay — Part 1*.

Albums

2013

Pure Heroine

The Love Club (EP)

Hit Singles

"Royals"

"Team"

"Tennis Court"

"Yellow Flicker Beat"

Works Consulted

Etheridge, Jess. "Singer now on centre stage." *North Shore Times*. February 8, 2013. http://www.stuff.co.nz/auckland/local-news/north-shore-times/8990736/Singer-now-on-centre-stage

Hoby, Hermione. "One to watch: Lorde." *The Observer*, June 29, 2013. http://www.theguardian.com/music/2013/jun/30/lorde-interview-royals-one-watch

Howard, Michael. "Lorde Signs a Publishing Deal for Millions." abcnews.com. November 14, 2013. http://abcnews.go.com/blogs/entertainment/2013/11/how-much-did-17-year-old-lorde-sign-a-publishing-deal-for/

"Katy Perry talks Lorde." TVNZ.co.nz. October 31, 2013. http://tvnz.co.nz/breakfast-news/katy-perry-talks-lorde-video-5666355

Ledonne, Rob. "Q & A: The Teenage Singing Sensation Lorde on Overnight Stardom." *The New York Times Style Magazine*. August 29, 2013. http://tmagazine.blogs.nytimes.com/2013/08/29/q-a-the-teenage-singing-sensation-lorde-on-overnight-stardom/?_r=

Lewis, Kasey. "Get to Know Lorde, the 16-Year-Old Pop Star Everyone's Talking About." *Teen Vogue*. http://www.teenvogue.com/entertainment/music/2013-07/lorde-interview

"Lorde features on Typhoon Haiyan charity album." 3News.com. November 26, 2013. http://www.3news.co.nz/Lorde-features-on-Typhoon-Haiyan-charity-album/tabid/418/articleID/322873/Default.aspx

"Lorde: I said no to Katy Perry's world tour." *The New Zealand Herald*. September 18, 2013. http://www.nzherald.co.nz/entertainment/news/article.cfm?c_id=1501119&objectid=11126715

McCarthy, Lauren. "Teen Queen: Lorde Takes New York." *Women's Wear Daily*. August 9, 2013. http://www.wwd.com/eye/people/teen-queen-lorde-takes-new-york-7084070

Nicks, Denver. "'Royals' Singer Lorde Caught in Racism Row." *Time Entertainment*. October 9, 2013. http://entertainment.time.com/2013/10/09/royals-singer-lorde-caught-in-racism-row/#ixzz2kxbzQutl

Petridis, Alexis. "Lorde: 'I'm just a freak.'" *The Guardian*. October 10, 2013. http://www.theguardian.com/music/2013/oct/10/lorde-just-freak-royals-pure-heroine?CMP=twt_gu

Stern, Marlow. "Meet Lorde, the 16-Year-Old Singer Poised to Take Over Pop Music." *The Daily Beast*. July 22, 2013. http://www.thedailybeast.com/articles/2013/07/22/meet-lorde-the-16-year-old-singer-poised-to-take-over-pop-music.html

Stoeffel, Kat. "Meet Lorde, the Teen Pop Star With a No Selfies Policy." *The Cut*. June 26, 2013. http://nymag.com/thecut/2013/06/meet-lorde-the-teen-pop-star-with-no-selfies.html

Von Glinow, Kiki. "Lorde's Real Name Is Not Lorde." *The Huffington Post*. October 21, 2013. http://www.huffingtonpost.com/2013/10/21/lorde-real-name_n_4138246.html

Weiner, Jonah. "Lorde's Teenage Dream." *Rolling Stone.* October 28, 2013.
http://www.rollingstone.com/music/news/lordes-teenage-dream-20131028#ixzz2odjkL68d

Yelich-O'Connor, Ella. "Our Lady Lorde: The Kiwi schoolgirl turned pop Royalty." Stuff.
co.nz. September 29, 2013. http://www.stuff.co.nz/entertainment/music/9208190/
Our-Lady-Lorde-The-Kiwi-schoolgirl-turned-pop-Royalty

On the Internet

Lorde Official Web Site

http://lorde.co.nz

GLOSSARY

accusation (ak-yoo-ZAY-shun)—A claim that someone has committed a fault; done wrong.

anonymity (an-noh-NIH-mih-tee)—The state of being unknown to people.

aristocrats (uh-RIH-stoh-kratz)—Members of a ruling class; royalty.

compilation (kom-pih-LAY-shun)—Assembling items together, such as songs by various music artists for one album.

Cristal—Brand-name champagne.

critique (krih-TEEK)—A detailed assessment.

debut (day-BYOO)—A first public appearance on stage, television, and the like.

imperialistic (im-peer-ee-uh-LIST-ik)—The policy of extending a nation's power by gaining territory.

inequity (in-EH-kwih-tee)—Unfairness.

influential (in-floo-EN-shull)—A person whose actions and opinions strongly change the course of events.

luxe (LUX)—Luxury; elegance.

Maybach (MAY-bok)—German luxury car.

vintage (VIN-tij)—Old; classic.